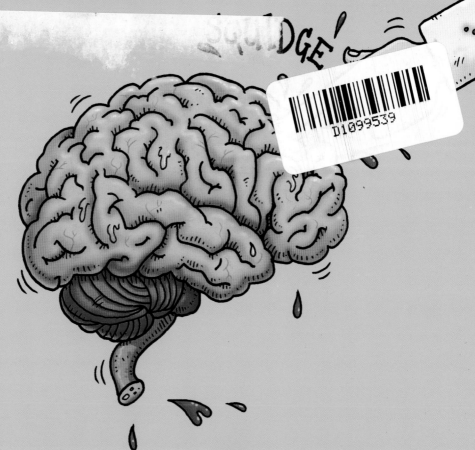

Bulging Brain
EXPERIMENTS

Nick Arnold

Illustrated by **Dave Smith**

www.horrible-science.co.uk

Visit Nick Arnold at
www.nickarnold-website.com

Scholastic Children's Books,
Euston House, 24 Eversholt Street,
London, NW1 1DB, UK

A division of Scholastic Ltd
London ~ New York ~ Toronto ~ Sydney ~ Auckland
Mexico City ~ New Delhi ~ Hong Kong

First published in the UK by Scholastic Ltd, 2008
This edition published by Scholastic Ltd, 2010

Text copyright © Nick Arnold, 2008
Illustrations by Dave Smith, based on the style of the original
Horrible Science artwork by Tony De Saulles
Illustrations © Dave Smith 2008
All rights reserved

ISBN 978 1407 11216 9

Printed and bound by Imago

2 4 6 8 10 9 7 5 3 1

CONTENTS

WELCOME!

INTRODUCTION

For years there have been scary rumours about the sinister castle in the dark wood. The locals whisper that the owner, famous scientist Baron Frankenstein, has created a monster boy from bits of body. But no one dares ask the Baron if the stories are true. Then one stormy night, a spine-tingling scream rings out from the castle. It's followed by a sickening slurping sound like ancient custard being tipped from a giant jar. What's going on? Dare you find out?

AGGGH! MONSTER BOY'S BRAIN HAS BLOWN UP!*

SQUELCH

ALAS, MONSTER BOY WAS PLAYING AN ESPECIALLY TRICKY LEVEL 33 VAMPIRE-ZAPPER GAME ON HIS SKULLBOX PLAYSTATION. I WARNED HIM IT WAS BAD FOR HIS BRAIN. I SAID IT WOULD BLOW HIS MIND – AND IT DID! AND WHAT'S MORE, THE FOOLISH BOY BLEW UP HIS PLAYSTATION TOO!!

*Scientific note – brains don't normally do this.

The Baron knows there's only one thing he can do. He has to fit Monster Boy with a new brain – and he needs to test the new brain to make sure it's working. Fortunately the Baron always keeps spares...

I HAVE THE BRAINS FOR THE JOB!

And that, dear reader, is where you come in. Your task is to help the Baron test the brain. And if you survive this book (and don't bank on it) you'll be a fully qualified Horrible Brain Scientist – licensed to shock your sister and bother your brother with your nasty knowledge. So let's do it!

YOU'LL BE NEEDING THIS!

SQUELCH

DRIP

READ THIS ON PAIN OF DEATH!

EVEN HORRIBLE SCIENTISTS DON'T WANT TO GET KILLED. SO YOU'D BETTER FOLLOW THESE RULES.

HE'S CRAZY BUT HE'S NOT KIDDING...

1 Don't perform your brain experiments on little brothers and sisters (when anyone is looking).

2 Read the instructions first. Make sure you have all the necessary bone saws, scalpels, blood buckets, etc. Clear away any valuable items, family pets and little brothers and sisters before you start.

3 Younger readers must recruit an adult assistant for any difficult cutting. You can play some music so that when the adult injures themselves their screams won't upset the neighbours.

4 Always clear up afterwards. Even I have to do this; although those bloodstains do take some shifting...

THE SQUISHY BRAIN

ON TEST! HANDS OFF B.F.

SQUELCH A BRAIN

BEWARE MESSY EXPERIMENT!

Wear your oldest clothes, put newspaper down and get ready to mop up afterwards!

I ALWAYS GIVE A BRAIN A GOOD SQUISH TO TEST ITS WATER CONTENT. A HEALTHY BRAIN SHOULD BE AS WATERY AS A POTATO – THAT'S ABOUT 80 PER CENT.

WHAT YOU NEED:
- **A human brain**

If you don't have one, you'll need the following:
- **Salt**
- **Instant potato flakes**
- **Spoon for mixing**
- **Two large freezer bags (ideally ones that you can seal, such as ziplock bags)**
- **Kitchen scales**
- **Measuring jug**
- **Red food colouring (not vital)**

WHAT YOU DO:

1 Measure 175 g of potato flakes and put them in one bag.

2 Add 400 g of salt.

3 Pour in 600 ml of hot water from the tap – BE CAREFUL! Hot water can scald you!

4 Feel free to add a couple of drops of blood … sorry, red food colouring into the jug. This will give your brain a cheerful pink colour. Be careful – food colour can stain fingers and clothes.

5 Place your bag of brain mixture inside the second bag – the blood makes it feel delightfully squashy. Squish the revolting mixture in the bag until it's thoroughly mixed.

WHAT HAPPENS:

CONGRATULATIONS! You're holding a blob that feels and weighs the same as a brain. You may like to sculpt it into a brain shape and let your family have a squish too.

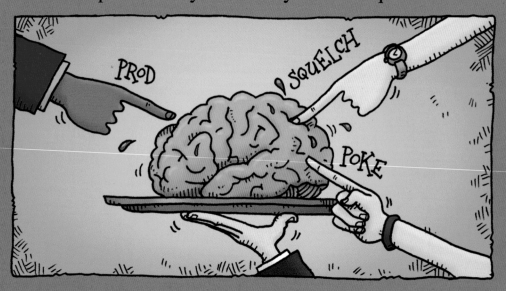

THIS IS BECAUSE:

The brain weighs about 1,280 g. A fresh brain is reddish-pink owing to the blood it contains. Stored brains get that well-known grey colour from billions of nerve cells or neurons. They're your brain's vital wiring – the stuff that you think with…

Bet you never knew!

Fresh brains pong like blue cheese. Feel free to add blue cheese to your brain mixture for that extra dash of realism. And if you fancy touching another brain, try prodding the top of a large mushroom. It feels frighteningly like a real brain.

POKE

OI – LEAVE IT!

THINKING CAP

The brain feels right and the Baron takes a closer look to check that it's got all the bits and pieces a brain needs. The brain is surprisingly complicated and you need a good brain to make sense of it. So is your brain up to the job?

IT'S ALL THERE!

IT'S A PITY HE'S NOT ALL THERE!

WHAT YOU NEED:
- An old white or flesh-coloured swimming cap
  (If you don't have one you could use
  half a plastic football or an old shower cap)
- Black waterproof felt pen
- Pink and red felt pens
- This book

WHAT YOU DO:

1 Draw the main parts of the brain on the cap like this…

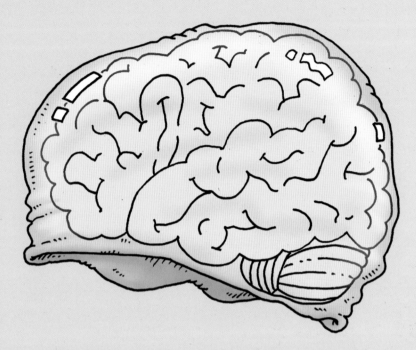

2 You could add a few red blood vessels and a lovely pink colour to give your brain a revoltingly realistic look. Er – hold on – you did make sure that the cap wasn't being used? If not your sister will be going swimming with a brain on her head.

3 Try the cap on. If you're feeling brave you could wear it to school and show your teacher that you really do have brains. And if you're especially brave you can claim to have suffered a terrible tin-opener accident and ask for the day off.

WHAT HAPPENS:

Your drawing of the brain bits should fit snugly over your own brain bits.

You may think that the brain looks weird but you haven't seen anything yet. The closer you look, the weirder it gets…

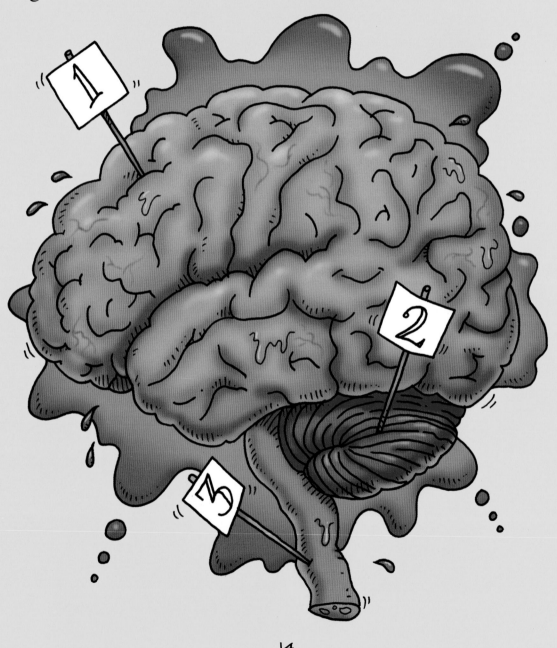

THIS IS BECAUSE:

You might think that your brain is very different (and far superior) to your little brother/sister's brain. But to be honest all brains look much the same. Here's what each brain bit does…

BOINGG!

1 Cerebrum

It's your most thoughtful body bit. You do your thinking and remember things in the outer layer known as the cortex. One part of the cerebrum, called the pre-frontal cortex, tells you not to do very naughty things. So if your brain's OK what's your excuse for being antisocial, Monster Boy?

2 Cerebellum

This bit controls and co-ordinates your movements, including the movements that you make when you know a job so well you don't have to think about it too much – like riding a bike.

3 Brain stem

This bit may not seem as exciting as the others, but it does control your heartbeat and breathing and other vital body functions. Without it life would be even less exciting – you would be dead!

WIRE UP YOUR BRAIN

This brain contains oodles of neurons – in all about 100 billion. Other cells are glial cells that feed the neurons and get rid of them when they die off.

TWIDDLE

FOCUS

As he peers down his microscope at the tangle of neurons in the Monster's new brain, the Baron can see the secret of its success. The neurons are linked together thousands of times to form a mind-blowing maze. Memories, thoughts and skills take the form of neuron pathways.

Can you make sense of your own amazing mind-maze?

WHAT YOU NEED:

• A piece of A4 paper (you can use a larger sheet of paper if you like) • A packet of felt pens or coloured pencils with at least ten colours

WHAT YOU DO:

1 Lay the paper on its side and draw the outline of a brain in tasteful pink.

2 Make a pair of ink blobs a few centimetres apart (each blob can be wherever you want in the brain shape. Make nine more ink blob pairs in different colours. (You can do more but you're just making work for yourself.)

3 Link a pair of blobs of the same colour with a line of the same colour. Now do this for every pair of coloured blobs.

4 Link every blob to every other blob using ink of the colour of the blob you are drawing the line to.

WHAT HAPPENS:

Confusing isn't the word for it! It's amazing how from just ten pairs of blobs you can create such a tremendous tangle of lines. Well, it's the same in your brain, and each of your 100 billion neurons can be wired to thousands more. In all there could be 100 TRILLION connections in your mind-blowing mind maze.

THIS IS BECAUSE:

You might think that your brother/sister has a brain the size of a stick insect, but in fact this awesome neuron network means that even tiny brains can handle dumper-trucks full of data. With processing power like this, who needs a computer?

Bet you never knew!

One hundred billion is a brain-boggling figure. Just think – if this book had 100 billon pages it would take you about 200,000 years to read it. Your gobsmacking giant book would be 8,000 km high and your bookshelf would stretch from London to San Francisco.

THE COPY OF 'BULGING BRAIN EXPERIMENTS' YOU BORROWED IS 50 YEARS OVERDUE... MIGHT YOU BE RETURNING IT ANYTIME SOON?

LIBRARY

THE BASHED-UP BRAIN

Delighted with the brain, the Baron makes plans to plop it inside Monster Boy's skull and wire up the nerves and blood vessels that will link it to the rest of the monster's body. But before he can start there's one more test to do. How will the brain cope with being shaken? Will this experiment leave you feeling shaken too?

FLAP

NOT YET, MONSTER BOY!

UNGH!

SPLOSH

WHAT YOU NEED:

- **Waterproof felt pen**
- **An egg**
- **An empty jam or honey jar and lid**

WHAT YOU DO:

1 Draw a face on the egg. (If this happens to look like your teacher, then blame your brain – NOT ME.)

2 Fill the jar to the brim with water.

3 Gently plop the egg in the jar. Replace the lid and shake the jar as much as you like.

4 Now repeat step 3 but without water. Shake the jar more g-e-n-t-l-y.

WHAT HAPPENS:

No matter how hard you shake your egg in the water, you'll find it very hard to crack. Without its cushioning of water, the poor old egg will crack very easily.

THIS IS BECAUSE:

The water is a shock absorber. It soaks up the force of the shaking and protects the egg from splatting in the jar. Your brain is cushioned in the same way by 150 ml of cerebrospinal (ser-ree-bro-spi-nal) fluid. Every time you move your head your brain actually sloshes around a bit, but at least you don't give yourself brain damage when you shake your head.

ACTUALLY, I DID THE TEST BY ROLLING THE BRAIN DOWN A STEEP HILL IN A COFFIN ON WHEELS...

WHEE!

SHOVE

BULGING BRAIN QUIZ

So how vast is your brain knowledge? This queasy quiz is sure to make your brain-box bulge... Put these creatures in order of brain weight, starting with the heaviest brain.

5 Bubbles the goldfish

1 Your little brother

 2 A sheep

6 A jellyfish

3 Your pet hamster

7 Your pet dog

4 A great white shark

8 An elephant

Answers:

8 An elephant's brain can weigh 5.5 kg.

1 That's about five times more than your little brother's brain.

2 A sheep brain weighs 140 g.

7 Your pet dog's brain weighs around 72 g.

4 A great white shark's brain only weighs 34 g.

3 Your hamster's brain is a pitiful 1.4 g.

5 But the puny brain of your goofy goldfish is 14 times lighter.

6 A jellyfish has no brain at all.

Larger beasts often have bigger brains – but not always. Great white sharks can weigh 1.2 tonnes but they have lighter brains than sheep. Mind you, having a heavy brain doesn't make you the greatest genius in the galaxy. You may think your little brother is more brainless than a half-witted jellyfish – but he's actually smarter than an elephant.

WEIRD WIRING

Monster Boy's new brain is now nestling happily between his ears and the Baron is busy testing its vital wiring – the nerves that control the monster's body and tell the brain what it's up to…

SPLIT PERSONALITY?

One of the most obvious things about Monster Boy's new brain – and your brain too, come to think of it – is that it's divided into two halves linked by a kind of nerve bridge.

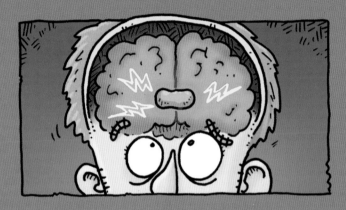

Does that mean you're in TWO minds about everything? Probably not. But it does mean that the left half of your brain looks after the right half of your body – and vice-versa. And it also means that one side of your brain tends to be in charge. The Baron wants to find out which side is the boss of Monster Boy's brain…

WHAT YOU NEED:

- **Yourself**
- **A piece of blank paper**
- **Notebook and pencil**
- **A good friend**
- **A radio**

WHAT YOU DO:

1 Divide your notebook into two columns with your name at the top of one and your friend's name at the top of the other.

2 Ask your friend to write their name on the piece of blank paper. If they hold their pen in their right hand, they're right-handed (well, knock me down with a wet brain). You can always check this finding by giving your friend a glass of their favourite drink (who says science is tough?). They'll probably pick it up with their "strong hand". Make a note of your results in your notebook.

3 Put the radio on fairly quietly in the next room. Ask your friend to listen to the radio by putting their ear to the wall. Make a note of which ear they use.

4 Now ask your friend (who is probably wondering what's going on) to walk upstairs. Note down which foot they use to take the first step.

5 Swap jobs and allow your friend to try these tests on you. I bet they'll like that…

I PUT **BOTH** EARS ON THE WALL…

WHAT HAPPENS:

You'll probably find that your friend will use the ear and foot on the same side as their writing hand.

THIS IS BECAUSE:

If you're right-handed the left side of your brain is in the driving seat and if you're left-handed it's the opposite way round. Since the bossy side of the brain controls the movements on the other side of the body you will probably prefer to use the ear and foot on that side too.

CRASH

PANG

IX VI

TINKLE

BASH

PACK IT IN, MONSTER BOY! YOU'LL WAKE THE DEAD! ...ACTUALLY, THAT COULD BE HANDY!

Bet you never knew!

About 90 per cent of us are right-handed and most of the rest are left-handed. But not all – some people are ambidextrous, which means they can use their left and right hands equally well. I guess it's hard to keep on the right side of them, ha ha!

ROTTEN REFLEXES

The Baron decides to test Monster Boy's reflexes. These are movements you make without thinking – like whipping away your hand when you touch something hot. All at once there's a sinister sizzle and a revolting aroma of burnt boy as the monster puts his hand too close to the candle flame…

FIZZZT

HMM – BETTER WORK ON THOSE REFLEXES!

So how good are your friend's reflexes?

WHAT YOU NEED:

- **A piece of paper**
- **A window**
- **A bright torch**
- **Your good friend from the previous experiment**

WHAT YOU DO:

1 Stand your good friend in front of the window with their face close to the glass.

2 Stand on the other side of the window. Screw the paper into a ball and suddenly chuck it at your friend's face.

3 If you and your good friend are still good friends, stand in front of them with your bright torch. Note the size of their pupils – these are the black circles at the centre of each iris. Shine the torch into one of their eyes.

WHAT HAPPENS:

When you throw the paper ball at your friend's face they should blink. With a bit of luck they might throw their hands in the air too. When you shine the light in their eyes, their pupils will shrink.

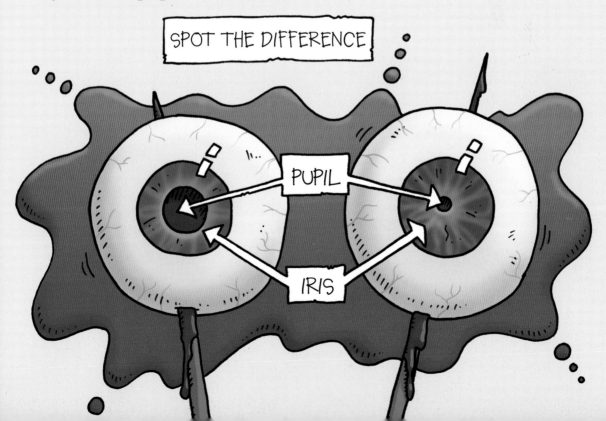

SPOT THE DIFFERENCE

PUPIL

IRIS

THIS IS BECAUSE:

MOST REFLEXES DON'T USE THE BRAIN – THE NERVE SIGNALS PASS THROUGH THE SPINAL CORD. AND NO REFLEX INVOLVES THINKING.

Blinking, throwing up your hands to your eyes when startled and shrinking of pupils in bright light are reflexes to protect your eyes. You need to act fast in an emergency, so it helps if you can make these movements without thinking. In fact, these reflexes are so important that they are used to test if people are dead.

Monster Boy withdraws his hand by reflex when caught stealing candied eyeballs.

YOINK

MONSTER BOY!

Bet you never knew!

I bet you won't believe this – but your EARS actually make sounds. Experts aren't sure what causes these mysterious noises but they may be due to nerve activity. Sadly you can't ever listen to your own musical lughole...

HE'S GOT A MUSICAL EAR.

THE LAUGHING BRAIN

Why in the name of horror is the Baron telling Monster Boy such a terrible joke?

Well, one of your most pleasurable reflexes is laughter; so the Baron is performing a vital brain test. Oh come on – you didn't think he was telling jokes for fun?

WHAT YOU NEED:

- **Your ever-trusty good friend**
- **A stopwatch or watch with a second hand**
- **A tape recorder (not vital)**
- **Notebook and pencil**

WHAT YOU DO:

1 Relax. I said r-e-l-a-x. It helps if you feel warm and comfortable. Take a deep breath – feeling relaxed now? OK – you can read on.

2 Find something to make you laugh. Our ever-helpful artist has added a cartoon to help. But if it doesn't work you could try asking your good friend to tickle you. And if that doesn't work you could ask a surgeon to give your friend a sense-of-humour transplant.

PRANCE

TWINKLE

WHAT ARE WE DOING?!

3 When you laugh your friend should note down:

• Whether you laugh with a "ha ha", "ho ho" or "he he" sound.
• How many sounds you make in a spell of laughing.
If your friend times your laughing they could estimate a sound-per-second score. This is easier if they can tape you laughing.

WHAT HAPPENS:

Scientists have found that people never make a mixture of sounds so you won't hear anyone going "ha he ho". While you're enjoying a good giggle you make about five sounds a second.

THIS IS BECAUSE:

Scientists reckon you laugh to relax and feel better. A good giggle can also prevent nasty situations from developing. Let's imagine a typical day at Rotten Road school.

Without laughter Mr Bunsen might have lost his temper and blown up the class in rage. Useful thing, laughter – as I'm sure you'll point out to your teacher next time you get told off for sniggering in class.

Bet you never knew!

1 In 1962 a teacher made a stupid remark at a school in Bobaku, in modern Tanzania. Nothing too strange about that – but within minutes the entire school was helpless with giggles. When the children got home their parents got the giggles too. Many people laughed until they were ill and the army had to close the school. No, this won't happen at your school, so stop grinning and carry on reading.

2 In fact, serious scientists take laughter very seriously. It's even got a scientific name – geleotology. Huh – trust a scientist to make a chuckle sound boring.

MONEY FOR NOTHING

YOUR REACTIONS ARE PAINFULLY SLOW. I CHALLENGE YOU TO CATCH THIS COIN.

DUH – WHAT COIN?

WHAT YOU NEED:

• A coin – if you don't happen to have a gold sovereign you could make do with a £1 coin. And if you don't happen to have £1 you could always borrow one from a gullible adult
• Your long-suffering good friend

WHAT YOU DO:

1 Balance the coin on your elbow like this…

2 Quickly turn your arm the right way round and try to catch the coin before it falls …
if you can!

3 Can your good friend do this?

WHAT HAPPENS: SNATCH

Well, hopefully both you and your friend can catch the coin. And even more hopefully you can spend the coin before the gullible adult catches up with you!

THIS IS BECAUSE:

You can catch the coin thanks to two reflexes that allow you to bend and straighten your arm very quickly. You may like to know that a nerve signal is a change in nerve chemistry that zooms along neurons in your brain at 483 km per hour. The signal leaps from cell to cell in the form of messenger chemicals. So I guess it really does help to keep your nerve…

CURIOUS BRAIN CURE QUIZ

Unusually for a scientist, the Baron is a keen believer in old-fashioned remedies. Some of the ancient remedies from the Baron's cure book sound very curious. But which sound too curious to be true?

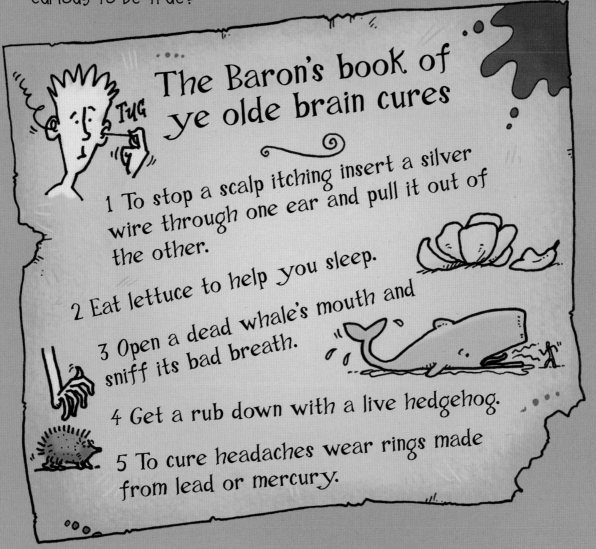

The Baron's book of ye olde brain cures

1 To stop a scalp itching insert a silver wire through one ear and pull it out of the other.

2 Eat lettuce to help you sleep.

3 Open a dead whale's mouth and sniff its bad breath.

4 Get a rub down with a live hedgehog.

5 To cure headaches wear rings made from lead or mercury.

Answers:

1 FALSE and don't try this at home or you could wind up a teeny-weeny bit dead.

2 TRUE – Roman emperors tried this. Well, at least it was healthy.

3 Amazing but TRUE. Sailors used to do this, and I bet they had a whale of a time (not).

4 FALSE – Hedgehog?! Don't be silly! They used a live pig! It was meant to cure epilepsy – a condition that causes fits. But it didn't work.

5 TRUE – and this is odd because lead and mercury are poisonous metals that can cause brain damage.

THE ALL-SEEING BRAIN

I bet you think that your eyeballs "see" things. They don't – all they do is detect light. It's your brain that makes sense of the signals from your eyeballs to tell you what you're seeing. The Baron is testing how well Monster Boy's brain can do this. Will the new brain prove to be a sight for sore eyes?

JUDGE FOR YOURSELF

Your brain is more than a squelchy thinking box – it's a judge. It can make up its own mind about a distance…

HOW FAR AWAY IS THIS FINGER?

WHAT FINGER?

OH DEAR!

WHAT YOU NEED:
- **Blu tak or modelling clay**
- **Paperclip**
- **Pencil**

WHAT YOU DO:

1 Make a blob of Blu tak and stick it to a table top.

2 Make the paperclip into a loop as shown and stick it in the Blu-tak blob…

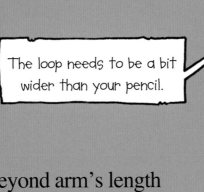

The loop needs to be a bit wider than your pencil.

3 Sit a bit beyond arm's length to the paper clip. Close one eye and try to push the end of the pencil through the loop.

4 Try this test with the closed eye open and the opened eye closed. And finally with both eyes open.

WHAT HAPPENS:

It's quite difficult to get the pencil through the loop with the aid of just one eye.

THIS IS BECAUSE:

Each of your eyeballs sends your brain a slightly different version of the loop in relation to its background. Your brain puts the pictures together to make a 3-D view from which to judge distance. The only way to do this with one eye is to move your head quickly from side to side.

Bet you never knew!

Look at a still object against a large moving background and your baffled brain thinks the still object is moving. Not convinced? Try peering at the moon on a cloudy, windy night. The moon seems to fly through the sky but it's only the clouds moving…

GOING DOTTY

THAT PEANUT-BRAINED MONSTER IS SEEING SPOTS IN FRONT OF HIS EYES. HE WON'T SEE ANY WITH THIS EXPERIMENT.

WAVE

WHAT YOU NEED:

• Pale pink or white paper • Pale grey paper (any other pale colour will do and if you haven't got coloured paper you could use felt pens on white paper) • Greaseproof paper – the same size as the pink paper • Ruler • Scissors

WHAT YOU DO:

1 Cut a 2.5-cm circle of pale grey paper. Younger readers should order an adult to do the cutting.

2 Place the light grey circle on the pink paper.

3 Lay the papers on a table in good light. Pull out a length of greaseproof paper and hold it a few centimetres away from the paper. You'll know you're holding the greaseproof paper at the right distance when you see the grey circle as a light vague blur.

4 Stare to one side of the blur (not at the blur itself). Make sure you don't move your eyes or head.

WHAT HAPPENS:

The blur seems to fade away. But that's IMPOSSIBLE! Where's it got to?

THIS IS BECAUSE:

Normally your ever-active eyeballs are busy checking the outline of a shape to tell your brain if it's moving. But your brain isn't too good at clocking blurred shapes – especially if they don't move…

LOOK WHAT HAPPENED WHEN I LET MONSTER BOY INTO A FOGGY GRAVEYARD AT NIGHT...

AGGH – WHO LEFT THAT TOMB THERE!

THUMP

NOW THAT'S WHAT I CALL A "GRAVE MISTAKE". OH WELL, AT LEAST YOUR BRAIN IS GREAT AT NOTICING SHAPES WITH NICE SHARP EDGES.

OH LOOK, MONEY!

GRR – THAT'S MINE!

AT THE DOUBLE

The Baron is bothered. Deeply madly bothered. Monster Boy seems to be seeing double – is there something seriously wrong with his new brain? It's definitely bad news…

ESPECIALLY WHEN HE WANTS TWO SUPPERS AND DOUBLE POCKET MONEY!

Can you see double and put it right at the double?

WHAT YOU NEED:

• Your brain
• Two pieces of A4 paper
• Scissors and sticky tape
• Ruler
• A pale wall (if you don't have a pale wall you could stick a large piece of white paper to the wall)

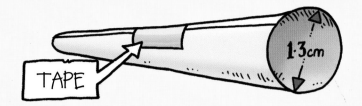

WHAT YOU DO:

1 Roll each piece of paper tightly. The open centre of each roll should be about 1.3 cm across. Secure each roll with sticky tape to stop it coming apart at the wrong moment.

OW!

HOLD ON, I'LL GET YOU ANOTHER EYE!

2 Put one roll to each eye and gaze at the pale wall.

3 You should see two circles. (If you can't see two circles you need to see an eye doctor and if you can't see the eye doctor then you probably can't see anything.)

4 Anyway, next you need to move the two circles together. Notice what happens to the brightness of each circle.

5 Now repeat steps 3 and 4 – but this time squash the roll to make a flattened circle something like the outline of an eye. Check what happens to the circle that you see when the two shapes merge together.

WHAT HAPPENS:

At step 4, as you move the tubes together, the circles seem to join and become brighter. Then you see a single circle as bright as the first two circles you saw. At step 5 you might see just one shape – or perhaps a blend of two. So why is this? Read on to find out!

THIS IS BECAUSE:

Your brain never stops trying to make sense of what you see – if it didn't you might think your mum is a streetlamp and the cat is a moth-eaten furry hat…

VERY FUNNY, MONSTER BOY.

SIGH

Your baffled brain thinks that the two bright circles should be brighter than one, so it sees the circles get brighter as they merge. But when you see the circles together they appear dimmer because your brain thinks they're just one boring old circle.

As for the changing shapes in step 5, that's all to do with which side of your brain is the stronger (see page 25). When each eye views a different image, your brain only sees the image from the stronger eye. Some brains, though, merge the two shapes...

NOW THAT GIVES ME AN IDEA FOR AN EVIL EXPERIMENT!

Monster Boy merged with the cat.

TIME I WAS GONE...

Bet you never knew!

If one part of the brain gets damaged, another part can sometimes take over the job. When Indian/US scientist Mriganka Sur linked up a baby ferret's eyeballs to the part of its brain that handled hearing, the ferret could still see a bit.

LOST ANY BODY BITS?

One of the more embarrassing problems of having a body made of other people's body bits is that some bits can drop off at inconvenient moments and turn up under the sofa or in the cat's bowl. So it's vital that Monster Boy's new brain knows where his body bits are.

How clued up is your brain?

WHAT YOU NEED:

• **Yourself and two hands**
(it helps if the hands actually belong to you)

WHAT YOU DO:

1 Hold your right hand over your head. Try to hold it really still – just imagine you're doing a very convincing waxwork impression.

2 Close your eyes and try to touch your nose with your left index finger.

3 Next try to touch your right thumb with your left index finger.

4 Keep going! Repeat steps 2 and 3 until you've touched each finger on your right hand with your busy left index finger. Then switch hands.

WHAT HAPPENS:

So how did you get on? Hopefully you managed to touch your nose and fingers without sticking a finger in your eye or up your left nostril and giving yourself a nasty nosebleed.

SPURT

WHAT WENT WRONG?

THIS IS BECAUSE:

Your body's muscles, tendons, joints and even the inner bits of your ears have sensors* that detect where they are and what they're up to. This info goes to your brain. So thanks to your brilliant brain and super sensors you've got a good idea what your body's up to…
* They're called proprioreceptors
(pro-pree-o-re-cep-tors)

I CAN'T MAKE SENSE OF WHAT HE'S UP TO…

WOBBLE

SPIN

JUGGLE

Bet you never knew!

If you ever munch a brain you might notice a greasy, fatty taste. In fact your brain is about 12 per cent fat, but that's nothing to do with eating too many sweets. It's because your neurons are lined with a fatty substance called myelin. The marvellous myelin works like the insulation round an electrical cable to stop the vital electrical signals from leaking out.

BAFFLING BRAIN BREAKFAST QUIZ

Talking about scoffing brains, can you believe that some otherwise sane people actually do this? What are these people up to and do they have a screw loose upstairs?

1 Why did women in Papua New Guinea eat their relatives' brains?

2 Why did explorer Douglas Mawson dine on dog brain in 1911?

3 Why did Tokeru Kabayashi eat 57 cow's brains in 2003?

4 Why do some people in the Far East scoff live monkey brains?

WARNING!

One of these answers is NOT needed!
a) There was nothing else to eat.
b) To honour a dead person.
c) Deliberate cruelty.
d) To boost brainpower.
e) Speed-eating record.

Answers:

1 b) In the 1950s this was common amongst the Fore people. The wretched women developed a deadly disease called kuru that ate away their brains.

2 a) He was exploring Antarctica and lost most of his food. He had to eat every last scrap of his sledge dogs, including the paws and brains, to stay alive. You may like to know that the brain was one of the tastiest bits.

3 e) He did it in 15 minutes. I wonder what he ate for pudding?

In fact, brains are considered a great delicacy in many parts of the world. In Samoa, for example, people enjoy pig brains baked in banana leaves, and in Austria fried calf brains and eggs are a tasty treat. Anyone hungry?

4 c) It's said the monkey sits at the table with the top of its head missing. The diners dip their chopsticks into the brain and tuck in.

Spare answer **d)** Eating brains won't make you brainy so leave your teacher's brain alone!

HORRIBLE HEAD-SPINNERS

When it comes to "seeing" with your brain, what you see is NOT what you get. In fact, your brain is easily bamboozled. Just look what happens to Monster Boy…

SINISTER SIGHTS

Monster Boy is looking at this book when something gives his new brain a nasty turn. Will you be freaked out too? Or can your brain grasp the grisly truth?

WHAT YOU NEED:

- **This book**
- **Your eyeballs (two ought to be enough)**
- **Photo or picture of a skyscraper or block of flats**
- **Ruler and pencil**
- **Scissors**

WHAT YOU DO:

1 What's this? Is it Count Dracula's skull or a very brave girl exploring a cave?

2 And what about this? Who has put a cloth over the blood splats on Baron Frankenstein's operating table?

3 For the next stage of the experiment you need to draw four vertical lines down the photo of the building and cut along them. As usual, younger readers need an adult to do the cutting.

4 Put your strips of photo together like this…

WHAT HAPPENS AND WHY:

When you look at the picture in step 1 as usual your brain is doing its best to make sense of what you see. But what if you could be seeing one of two things? Well, your mind can't make up its mind. So you see first one thing then the other.

In step 2 there wasn't actually a cloth over the blood splats. It's just a faded area of each splat that your ever-helpful brain tries to fit together to make a rectangle.

Does your building in step 3 look set to tumble? Blame your brain! It orders your eyeballs to follow lines. The windows form horizontal and vertical patterns that your brain puts together to make ... wobbly lines!

Did this experiment leave you a bit wobbly too? Monster Boy seems to have lost his head completely...

VILE VISIONS

When you watch something move, things can get even worse for your mixed-up mind. The Baron is testing this part of the monster's brainpower…

You might find this experiment quite moving…

WATCH THE BIRDY.

GWAWK!

IT'S RUDE TO STARE.

WHAT YOU NEED:
- A pen
- Photocopier
- Sticky tape and scissors
- Blu tak
- Pencil

WHAT YOU DO:

1 Photocopy or trace the picture below. If you like you can colour it in. Cut it out and fold it along the dotted line. Cut out hole A.

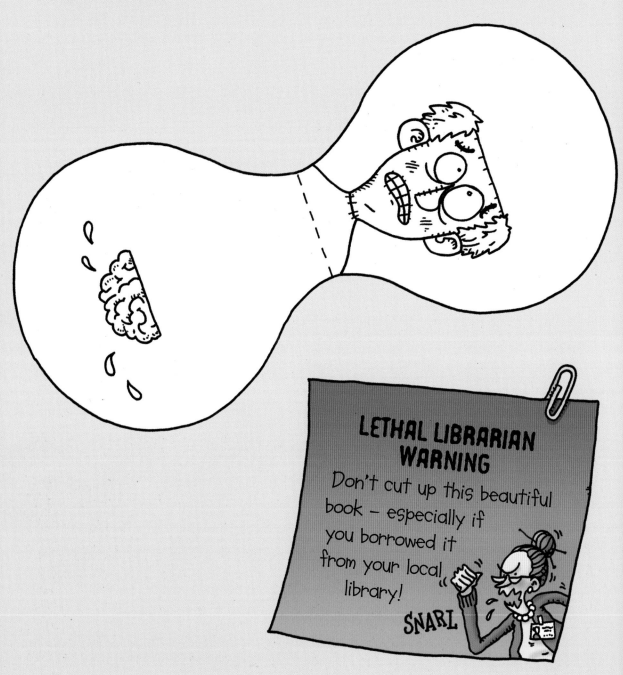

LETHAL LIBRARIAN WARNING

Don't cut up this beautiful book – especially if you borrowed it from your local library!

SNARL

2 Stick the card to the end of the pencil with Blu tak as shown. The point of the pencil should stick into the Blu tak.

3 Hold the pencil between your palms and roll it from side to side as fast as possible.

WHAT HAPPENS:
You'll see a tasteful image of Monster Boy with his brain showing.

THIS IS BECAUSE:
Your baffled brain can only work so fast. If it's shown more than 20 pictures a second, your brain blends them into a single picture. You may like to repeat the experiment with the curtains drawn. The dimmer the light, the longer your brain takes to make sense of the pictures.

Bet you never knew!
TV pictures are made up of a dot scanning the screen 50 times a second. It's fast enough to fool your brain that it's watching a moving picture when in fact you're looking at nothing half the time. And just think – that means you must spend two hours of an evening's viewing gazing vacantly at a blank screen!

HORRIBLE HANDS

Monster Boy is not known for his personal hygiene

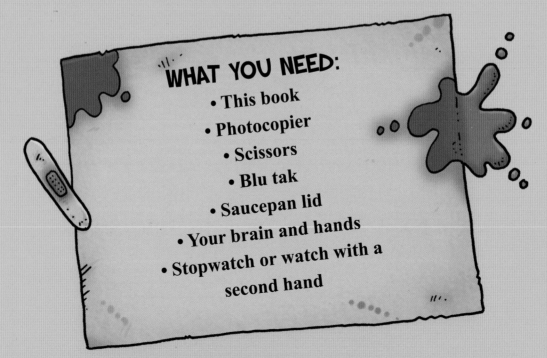

WHAT YOU NEED:
- **This book**
- **Photocopier**
- **Scissors**
- **Blu tak**
- **Saucepan lid**
- **Your brain and hands**
- **Stopwatch or watch with a second hand**

WHAT YOU DO:

1 Photocopy the pattern below. Cut out the circle from the photocopy.

2 Use Blu tak to stick the circle to the underside of the saucepan lid.

3 Spin the lid quite slowly on a flat smooth surface. Stare at the turning lid for 20 seconds under a bright light.

4 Now look at the palm of your hand from the same distance and under the same light.

WHAT HAPPENS:

Your palm appears to be moving just as if there were alien worms wriggling under your skin. It might even be turning in the opposite direction to the saucepan lid. Come to think about it – you can get this effect by looking at anything. Try looking at a scary model figure or your pet hamster…

THIS IS BECAUSE:

Your brain has two regions that sense things moving round – one for each direction.

One region of the monster's brain watches clock hands and another watches fly.

BUZZZ Z Z Z

WHIZZ

Both sets of neurons fire all the time – even when you're not looking at anything that moves. In the experiment one set of motion sensors fired faster and then slowed as they got used to the saucepan lid turning. When you looked at your palm, the other set were still firing at their normal speed and so you saw your palm moving. I hope it didn't make you sick!

SICK

PONG

Oh dear – it's too much for monster boy!

Bet you never knew!

In 2000, University of California scientists found that you can see things more clearly if they make a noise to grab your attention. Maybe that's why little kids are always screaming – or are they just attention-seekers?

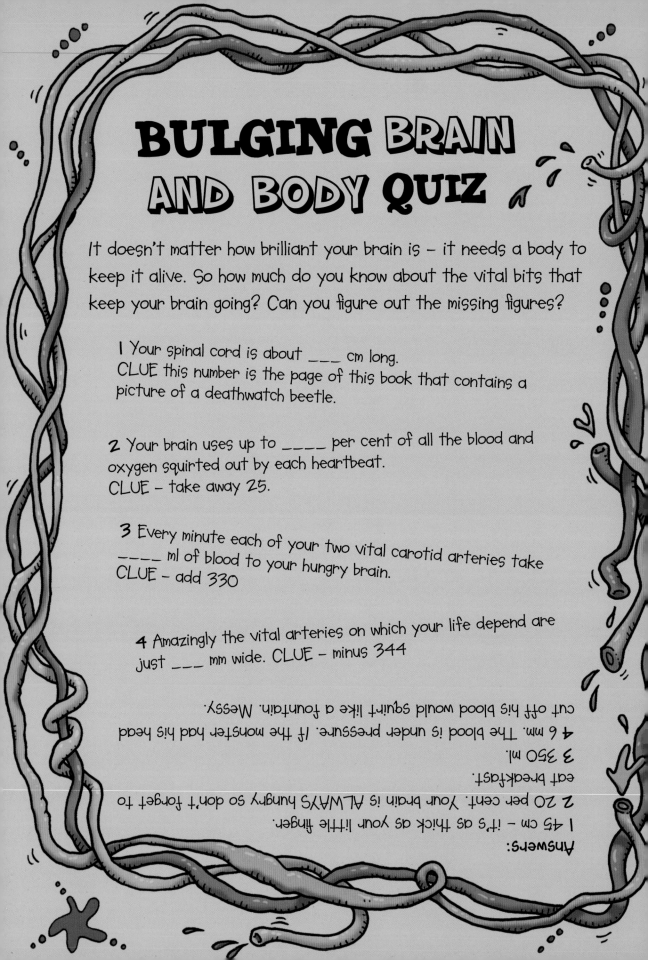

BULGING BRAIN AND BODY QUIZ

It doesn't matter how brilliant your brain is – it needs a body to keep it alive. So how much do you know about the vital bits that keep your brain going? Can you figure out the missing figures?

1 Your spinal cord is about ___ cm long.
CLUE this number is the page of this book that contains a picture of a deathwatch beetle.

2 Your brain uses up to ____ per cent of all the blood and oxygen squirted out by each heartbeat.
CLUE – take away 25.

3 Every minute each of your two vital carotid arteries take ____ ml of blood to your hungry brain.
CLUE – add 330

4 Amazingly the vital arteries on which your life depend are just ___ mm wide. CLUE – minus 344

Answers:

1 45 cm – it's as thick as your little finger.

2 20 per cent. Your brain is ALWAYS hungry so don't forget to eat breakfast.

3 350 ml.

4 6 mm. The blood is under pressure. If the monster had his head cut off his blood would squirt like a fountain. Messy.

BAFFLE YOUR BRAIN

After a good day's sleep and a restoring mug of hot choco-blood, Monster Boy is back to his old self. And not a moment too soon – the Baron is plotting some even more beastly brain-teasing trials for his clueless creation…

WHO NOSE?

Normally you can rely on your face not changing shape.
Well, you can can't you?

So how many noses have you got?

WHAT YOU NEED:

- **Your hand complete with fingers**
- **Your face (don't forget to check how many noses you've got first!)**

WHAT YOU DO:

1 Cross your index and third fingers so that the third finger is on top of the index finger. You may need to hold your fingers in position.

2 Place the "v" where the fingers cross over your nose.

3 Close your eyes and stroke your nose with the crossed fingers.

RUB

WHAT HAPPENS:

WOAH! Your boggled brain gets the impression that you've grown a spare schnozzle. What in the name of horrors is this?

THIS IS BECAUSE:

Your baffled brain can't get used to having your fingers crossed. So when it feels a nose to the left of one finger and the right of the other it naturally thinks it's feeling two noses.

BUT I FELT TWO NOSES!

I COULD ALWAYS SEW ON ANOTHER ONE...

ROTTEN READING

Having two noses is bad enough but learning the alphabet is about to prove a whole new nightmare for Monster Boy. Why, it's almost as bad as being back at ghoul school...

WHAT YOU NEED:

> **PERSONALLY I FIND THAT OFFENSIVE!**

- **Two pieces of paper**
- **Black felt pen**
- **Adult assistant (with less brains than a headless chicken)**

WHAT YOU DO:

1 Copy or trace drawing A on to one piece of paper. Copy or trace drawing B onto the second piece of paper.

A. TOJ

B. HAHOE

2 Hold your copy of drawing A horizontally and ask your friend what it says. If they're a zilch-brained zombie they'll say "DUH – I can't hear it say anything!" If they're a bit less stupid they'll say "TOJ". Now show drawing B and ask them to read what they see. They'll probably say "HAHOE".

WHAT HAPPENS:

Calmly inform your adult assistant that they've got it wrong not once but twice. And prove it by turning drawings A and B on end…

THIS IS BECAUSE:

Once more the poor old brain is only trying to make sense of things. This time it's using its memory of letters. It's in such a hurry to recognize the letters that it doesn't notice that it's reading them the wrong way up.

Bet you never knew!

A phobia is an overwhelming dread of something that makes the sufferer ill. There are dozens of fearsome phobias, including quite a few weird ones...

*English translations:
The Baron is ara-ky-bute-ro-fo-bic para-skay-dek-at-tree-a-fo-bic = scared of getting peanut butter stuck to the roof of his mouth on Friday 13th.

   Monster Boy is skol-ee-on-o-fo-bic so-fo-fo-bic = scared of learning at school.

   So is it worth trying a few phobias to get a day off school? Better not – otherwise you might suffer from rhabdophobia = rab-do-fo-bee-a = fear of being told off and beaten with a cane!

STRANGE STORIES

You might think that reading long words is harder than chewing a concrete toffee, but fortunately your brain is up to the job. Well, it must be because you're reading this highly educational brain-boosting book. So does that mean you're up for this terrible test? Or will you get your letters in a twist?

WHAT YOU NEED:

- **This book**
- **Your brain (a couple of eyeballs would also be handy to help you read the text)**

WHAT YOU DO:

1 This story was printed by a sensationally stupid zombie printer who made loads of mistakes. Can you read it?

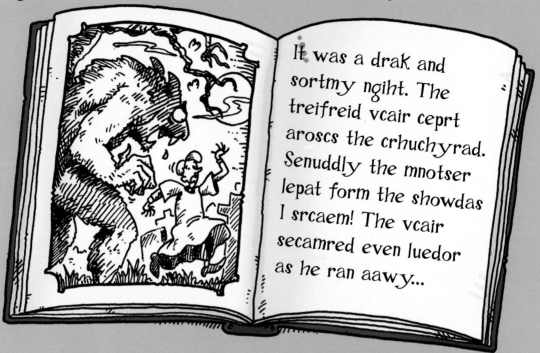

It was a drak and sortmy ngiht. The treifreid vcair ceprt aroscs the crhuchyrad. Senuddly the mnotser lepat form the showdas I srcaem! The vcair secamred even luedor as he ran aawy...

2 Good story, huh? Want to read the next page? Oh dear – it looks like the zonked-out zombie has forgotten to print the lower half of the words. Can you still make sense of it?

THE MONSTER WAS JUST ABOUT TO TURN ON THE VICAR WHEN HE HEARD A SQUEAK. LOOKING DOWN HE SAW A FURRY SHAPE – AAGH! YELLED THE MONSTER AS HE RAN AWAY. HE HAD NEVER SEEN A MOUSE BEFORE. THE END

WHAT HAPPENS:

If your spelling is as bad as the spelling on the first page you would be sent to the boottm of the calss. But oddly enough you can read the page without too much difficulty…

You probably thought you could read the second page of the story too. But you were WRONG. That zombie printer must have had a brainstorm because all you were reading was a mass of meaningless rubbish. It's true – here are the complete letters…

JUF MQNSJFB WAS THSJ
APQHJ JQ JUBN QN JUF
VIGAB WUFN UF UFABD
A SOHFAK. LQQKINC
DQWN UF SAW A EHBBX
SUARF – ACCU XFLLFD
JUF MQNSJFB AS UF BAN
AWAX. UF UAD NFVFB
SFFN A MQHSF RFEQBF.
JUE FND

THIS IS BECAUSE:

As you read this page your ever-busy eyeballs constantly scan sentences. And your brain doesn't so much read the letters as recognize the shape of the words and then try to make sense of each sentence. In step 1 the letters at the start and end of each word were where they should be and your brain did the rest. Mind you – that's no excuse for terrible spelling, as I am sure your teacher will remind you. Your ability to recognize words explains why you thought you could read the second page of the story. But in fact your brain was too brainy for its own good. It was so keen to read the words that it got the letters wrong. Cruel trick, that!

CONFUSING COLOURS

Monster Boy's bad night is about to get a whole lot worse. The Baron wants to test his young creation's brain using colours in a very confusing fashion. Can you conquer the confusing colours challenge?

WHAT YOU NEED:

• **A packet of coloured felt pens – you will need 11 different colours including black. If you're a high-tech horrible scientist you could use a computer with a colour printer. • A stopwatch or watch with a second hand • Your good friend or adult assistant**

I'VE GOT BLUE BLOOD!

WHAT YOU DO:

1 On a blank piece of paper write the following:
List 1 RED BLUE YELLOW GREEN… You need to write each word in the colour it describes, so RED needs to be written in RED, BLUE needs to be written in … yes, you've got the idea! Now carry on with: PURPLE ORANGE GREY PINK BLACK GREY RED WHITE YELLOW BROWN PURPLE BLUE. (You can write WHITE by outlining each letter in black.) If you're working on a computer you will need to change the font

colour for each word and highlight the word WHITE with a dark background.

2 Now hopefully your brain is switched on because this step is a touch more tricky. On your second sheet write: List 2: BLUE BLACK RED WHITE. But – and this is the interesting bit – you write the words in a different colour – so BLUE could be written in white, BLACK could be purple, RED could be brown and WHITE could be grey. You can complete your list with: GREY GREEN WHITE YELLOW WHITE PURPLE GREY BROWN YELLOW BROWN ORANGE PINK. You can write each word in any colour you like as long as it's not the colour the word describes. If you're working on a computer you will need to print out lists 1 and 2 and get ready to test your brain cells.

3 This bit's as easy as falling asleep in a science lesson. Ask your good friend to set the stopwatch while you read list 1 aloud. It doesn't matter whether you read it across or in columns – your job is to read the page as fast as you can. Finished? Ask your friend to jot down your time.

4 And now things get a bit harder. Take a look at list 2. You have to say what colour the words are. Got that? We're after the colours not what the words say! Once again, your friend should clock your time. Then you can swap jobs and note your friend's time for steps 1 and 3.

WHAT HAPPENS:

That last bit wasn't so easy was it? In fact, it can take twice as long to get through list 2. Or longer if you happen to be Monster Boy…

BLUE, NO, RED! AAGH!!

THE TEST SHOULD HAVE FINISHED TWO HOURS AGO.

IT WOULD HELP IF THE BOOK WEREN'T UPSIDE DOWN.

THIS IS BECAUSE:

The experiment is based on a famous psychology test (psychology = si-kol-o-gee = the study of the mind). It's called the Stroop test because John Ridley Stroop invented it in 1935. As usual your brain wants to make sense of things, and it's very happy when the columns match the words – in fact it works faster than usual. But when colours and words don't match, your brain keeps trying to read the word and then figure out why the colours don't match. Hence the delay.

Bet you never knew!

The more tired or angry you are, the longer the test takes. Older people take longer too. You could experiment on your elderly teachers but they might get angry and see red and then they'll never finish the test!

NUTTY NEWS QUIZ

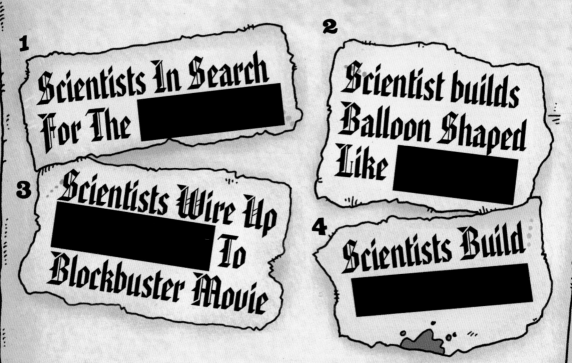

1 Scientists In Search For The ▬

2 Scientist builds Balloon Shaped Like ▬

3 Scientists Wire Up ▬ To Blockbuster Movie

4 Scientists Build ▬

Simply work out the missing words.
Missing words: Warning there is one extra! **a)** Locust brain **b)** Giant brain **c)** Tickle machine **d)** Funniest joke **e)** Green alien brain.

Answers: 1 d) US scientists were actually trying to find out what made people bad at their jobs. They found, among other things, that useless workers couldn't tell which jokes were funny. **2 b)** Imagine a brain the size of a nine-storey block of flats. It was the work of scientist Scott R Gibbs. **3 a)** The scientists from Newcastle University were trying to find out how locust brain-cells deal with moving images – so they showed the locust brain Star Wars. They used the data to create a robot brain that worked in a similar way. **4 c)** Scientists from University College built the tickle machine to find out why you can't tickle yourself. They found that you need to be surprised – as when someone else does the tickling. **Leftover answer e)** If you've seen one of these you may need your head examined.

TEST YOUR BRAIN CELLS

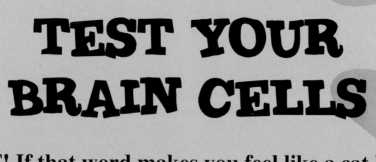

TEST! If that word makes you feel like a cat being taken to the vet then spare a thought for Monster Boy. The final phase of the Baron's experiments programme will test the brain to breaking point. Will Monster Boy's grey matter end up on the revolting reject pile?

DON'T COUNT ON IT!

Being able to work out sums in your head is one of your brainy brain's most awesome abilities. Mind you, some people think that mental arithmetic = mental torture.

HAVE YOU GOT A HEAD FOR FIGURES?

SCRATCH

DON'T COUNT ON IT!

Anyway, the monster's new brain is running hard. But the Baron's keen to up the pace a little with the ultimate challenge – remembering numbers. So how many phone numbers and birthdays can YOU recall? This experiment will convince your family you're a mathematical genius!

WHAT YOU NEED:

• This book • Paper and pencil • A diary or calendar for this year or next year • A gullible family

WHAT YOU DO:

1 First of all you need a reliable method of remembering numbers. Sounds tricky? Don't worry, here it is…

0 CAUGHT-SHORT

1 BUN-TUM

2 POO-SHOE

3 BEE-WEE

4 SORE-PAW

5 LIVE-HIVE

6 STICKY-SICK

7 KEVIN-HEAVEN

8 PLATE-CRATE

9 FINE-LINE

2 Read the list and picture the words in your mind.

3 Now look at the diary and write down the date of the first FRIDAY in each month. You should end up with 12 numbers.

4 Using your code, turn your numbers into a story. So, for example… 6 1 7 4 2 could be a sticky-sick bun sent Kevin to Heaven with a sore paw dipped in poo. IMPORTANT NOTE – the story doesn't have to make sense!

5 Once your story is stored in your memory, tell your family that thanks to your incredible mathematical genius you can calculate the exact day of the week for any date in the year (they may find this hard to believe).

WHAT HAPPENS:

If someone says "September 13th" all you do do is remember the numbers you memorized. The ninth number will be the date of the first Friday in September – then you count through the days in your head until you get to the 13th. Meanwhile your family think you're doing complex maths in your head.

THIS IS BECAUSE:

Your short-term memory can hold about seven numbers for a few seconds. But fortunately your brain finds it easier to remember pictures, especially when they're linked by a story. So by turning numbers into a story, it helps you remember them more easily.

How STUPID ARE YOU?

Are you smarter than the average chimp? Or are you a hamster brain who would swap your new playstation for a smelly pair of trainers and get lost in your back garden? The moment of truth has dawned…

WHAT YOU NEED:

• **This book**
• **Your ever-loyal good friend (hopefully they didn't run off when they saw the word TEST at the start of this chapter)**

WHAT YOU DO:

1 Ask your friend the following questions. You shouldn't tell your friend the correct answers until they've answered all the questions. Monster Boy is digging up six skeletons for one of the Baron's revolting experiments…

a) To dig up a skeleton the monster digs a hole 2 metres deep, 2 metres long and 1 metre across. How much earth is in the hole?

b) If Monster Boy digs up every single skeleton, how many are left?

c) DISASTER! Monster Boy is spotted! He's chased by a widow and her husband. Why is he scared?

d) A vicar and his dog join the chase. Which does the monster prefer to be attacked by – the vicar or the dog?

e) Monster Boy is trapped in an underground crypt. The vicar and his dog are blocking the only exit. How does he escape?

2 Now tell your friend the awful answers…

a) None – I told you that Monster Boy dug the earth from the hole.

b) Six – they're *married* skeletons, ha, ha!

c) The widow's husband must be dead – so he's a ghost!

d) Neither – he'd prefer not to be attacked.

e) Easy – the exit was barred so he escapes through the entrance!

WHAT HAPPENS:

EITHER your friend will get every answer wrong OR they'll get them all right. In which case they've read this book and you can disqualify them for cheating!

THIS IS BECAUSE:

When your brain tries to answer a question it makes a mental picture of the problem. But a trick question is designed to fool your brain into missing vital info. This is the sort of question a terrible teacher tortures their pupils with. By the end of the test your friend will be tearing their hair out … or tearing your hair out.

YES, MONSTER BOY, YOU ARE STUPID!

GRR!

OH-ER MONSTER BOY'S BRAIN IS GETTING UPSET!

Bet you never knew!

And talking about stupidity – violent head banging can be dangerous but some people do it for fun. Some rock fans have got dangerous brain clots because they shook their heads too hard to the beat of their favourite group.

STOP IT, MONSTER BOY, YOUR HEAD'S NOT ON PROPERLY!

STAKE THAT COFFIN

For days the Baron has been experimenting on Monster Boy's new brain. The poor brain has been squished and shaken, bemused and baffled, befuddled and muddled, mystified and mindwiped. But now Monster Boy's had enough and a mind memory test gets a bit too memorable… Are you ready to crack?

WHAT YOU NEED:

- Your good friend (that's if they're still a good friend and not a good enemy)
- Four sheets of 1-cm-squared graph paper
- Sticky tape and scissors
- Two sheets of paper and pencils
- Stopwatch or watch with a second hand

WHAT YOU DO:

1 Stick two sheets of graph paper together with sticky tape to make an A3 sheet. Then do the same for the other two sheets of paper.

2 Next you need to draw ten coffins complete with vampires somewhere on your sheet of paper. Each coffin needs to be 3 cm by 1 cm across. Here's one for you to copy. Your friend should do this for the other sheet of paper.

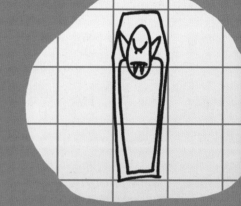

3 Now for the memory test. When you and your friend have finished you can allow each other FIFTEEN seconds to study your coffin plans. Make sure they don't take a split-second longer than 15 seconds! Can you remember where their coffins are?

4 Write 1 in the top left-hand square of your sheet, and 2 in the square on its right. Continue to number the squares along the top. Write A in the top left hand square and continue to letter all the squares down the left-hand side of the sheet. Your friend should number and letter their sheet in the same way. Make sure you don't peep at your friend's coffins and make extra-sure they don't take a crafty look at yours!

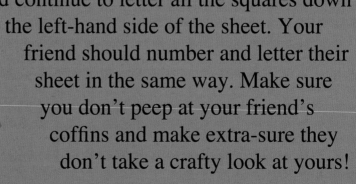

VAMPIRE STAKEOUT GAME RULES

As every clued—up vampire hunter knows, the only way to stop a beastly bloodsucker is to drive a stake through its heart — and I mean a pointed wooden pole and not the food you eat with onions and chips. In this game you can do just that, but be warned: you're playing for very high, er, stakes...

1 Toss a coin to decide whether you or your friend starts. Take it in turns to call out a square on the other player's board — for example A6.

2 To finish off a vile vampire, you need to hit their heart — that's the middle square of each coffin. If you hit their head or feet your friend must call out "HIT!" and if you hit the heart they can call out "STAKE—OUT!" If you miss they call out "FANGS A LOT!"

3 Now for more memory testing. When a player calls out a square the other player needs to write down the coordinates of that square. If the other player calls out the same square later on they miss a go. So you need to remember which squares you are calling. (Make sure your friend doesn't write down the squares they are calling — this is called "cheating".)

4 The winner is the first player to wipe out the other player's vampires. Oh, and by the way, if by the end of the game you fail to finish off any of the vampires you hit you will get KILLED by the angry undead. OH—ER!

WHAT HAPPENS AND WHY:

It's quite hard to remember where the coffins are and what squares you called out. This is because the game is quite distracting and there's lots of info to take in. What's more, scientists have found that stress makes it harder for you to remember anything and playing the game might be stressful. And it's at this stressful moment that Monster Boy loses his rag…

OH NO! Has the Baron had his stake and chips? Will he end up as a skewered scientist? I'll tell you after the quiz…

COULD YOU BE A BRAIN EXPERT?

So, is your amazing brain amazingly brainy enough to tackle the most cerebrum-crunching challenges in science?

1 Can a person hear the blood pulsing in their own brain?
a) Yes, but only if the blood vessels are damaged.
b) No way.

2 Is there really a disease called "alien hand syndrome"?
a) Yes, it's when your hand turns green.
b) Yes, it's when your hand takes on a life of its own and tries to strangle you.

STRUGGLE

LASH

BARON – WHERE DID MY NEW HAND COME FROM?

3 Can your brain see a ghostly image of yourself?
a) Yes.
b) There's no such thing as ghosts!

4 I know you don't believe this but there really is a disease called "crocodile tears". What does this disease do to you?
a) You go round biting people and bursting into tears.
b) When you sniff your dinner you cry instead of dribbling.

Answers:

1 a) In 1928 a patient in Boston, USA, complained of a rushing sound. It grew worse when he tried to read. Dr John Fulton listened to the man's brain, exposed after a botched op and heard the sound. It was the blood rushing in the visual area of the man's brain.

2 b) Yes, it happens when patients have the nerves linking the two halves of their brain cut. Each half tries to do the opposite of the other – for example the right side wants to close a door when the left is trying to open it. There have been cases of victims trying to strangle themselves with one hand.

3 a) Experts call this the autoscopic illusion. Your sense of where you are gets muddled with the part of the brain that sees things. So you think you can see yourself. One man spent hours making faces at his "ghost".

4 b) It's caused by damage to the nerves that control your salivary glands (where spit is made) and tear glands. Instead of making you dribble the nerve signals trigger tears.

EPILOGUE
IT MAKES YOU THINK!

Bet you thought that Monster Boy drove that stake into Baron Frankenstein's heart? Let's check out Monster Boy's brain.

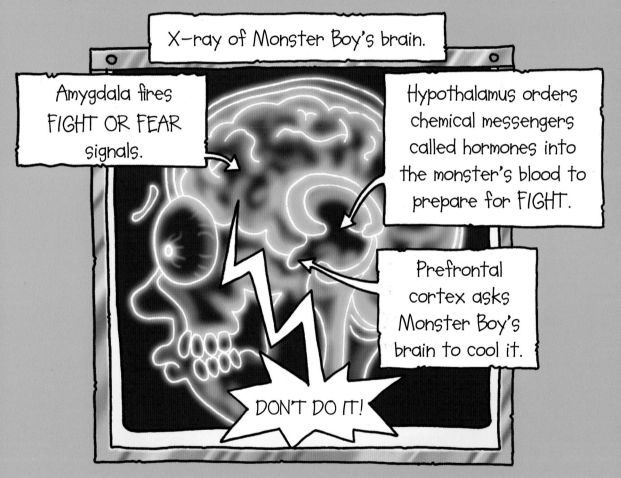

X-ray of Monster Boy's brain.

Amygdala fires FIGHT OR FEAR signals.

Hypothalamus orders chemical messengers called hormones into the monster's blood to prepare for FIGHT.

Prefrontal cortex asks Monster Boy's brain to cool it.

DON'T DO IT!

Fortunately Monster Boy's new brain can control his temper. Monster Boy calms down and for once the Baron is trying to be nice to his creation…

That's the good thing about your brain – it gives you feelings and then helps you control them. It gives you choices and helps you make the right ones. And that's not all.

For years your brain sits quietly in your skull without even a squelch or a gurgle. It looks as exciting as cold, lumpy porridge. But it's busy all the time, and within its intricate network of nerves and blood vessels are your innermost secrets, your dreams and memories. You can't lift a finger without your brain, but with it you're a complete human being. And you can do anything – including trying the experiments in this book and becoming a Horrible Brain Scientist. You can even play a computer game…